MW01227215

ABOLITIONIST TRAINING 101

30-DAY SEX TRAFFICKING EDUCATIONAL GUIDEBOOK

Written by

Dana and Lena Parriera

ISBN: 9798506846741

TABLE OF CONTENTS

TABLE OF CONTENTS

BONUS MATERIAL

Becoming an Abolitionist

The term *abolitionist* comes from the mentality of abolishing something unhealthy in a society. For us, we long to *abolish* slavery. Bondage in any form is unacceptable; slavery is rampant and requires individuals willing to fight for victims trapped, traded, and caught up in captivity. We need advocates to join the movement and assist in ending slavery. For that to happen, it's essential to understand what drives the sex industry and become an advocate for those trapped in slavery. For **30 DAYS,** you will learn about all the surrounding aspects of slavery, with a heavy focus on sex trafficking. To combat this struggle, it is essential first to understand what fuels this issue and what can be done to end it. When you join the movement and reveal the message of truth and freedom to others, you become an advocate for those who are enslaved. By joining, you become a part of the solution. We hope you will be educated in all truth as you heroically face the challenges of becoming an advocate for the voiceless.

Donate to Help Fight!

Fund the fight for freedom. Get sponsors, start a fundraising campaign, and invite friends to join the movement. We can't do this alone! You can be a massive help in ending human sex trafficking! Donate to **ISA**, which will go directly to fighting sex trafficking locally and globally through prevention and intervention.

Please visit www.ISAFreedom.org for more information.

WHAT IS TRAFFICKING?

Modern-day slavery has been termed 'trafficking' because it shows the different aspects of mobility in this global trading society. Never before have we been so vastly connected due to travel and the internet. Now online activities create a whole new demand, previously never seen in the history of the world.

This is the ability to visualize what is being offered and consume more than ever. Because of accessible connections with people all over the world, a new problem has been created. And that is the advancement of slavery. With more demand comes more enslaved people.

This is why we have more slavery today than ever before.

All **TRAFFICKING** is a form of slavery.

JOT YOUR JOURNEY

QUESTION: How big do you think our slavery problem is? Do you think that we have many enslaved people today?

_____

_____

_____

ANSWER: *It is believed that 4.9 million slaves were taken from Africa hundreds of years ago, which was over 300 years. According to the U.N. and ILO, we have over 40.3 million slaves today. Experts say that we can double our estimated number of slaves in our present-day... since it is impossible to get accurate numbers because it is an underground activity that scarcely reaches the light.*

⭐ ⭐ ⭐

QUESTION: Did you know that there are more slaves today than in our past history? Why do you think this is?

_____

_____

_____

ANSWER: *There is a higher demand for products and services from people throughout the world. We have a commodity-driven society. Humans are commonly viewed as products by providing service, sex, or material production. This creates a huge demand for slaves.*

TYPES OF
TRAFFICKING

★ ★ ★

There are many types of trafficking, including labor, pregnancy, bride, sex, debt bondage, domestic servant, beggar, organ, and many more forms of modern-day slavery. All slavery is wrong and goes against fundamental human rights.

All types of trafficking take advantage of the person under another's authority.

Today, those enslaved by traffickers are used just like slaves of old. Modern-day slaves are treated unkindly, abused in all forms, forced to make a profit for those that control them, and expendable in various ways to those that capitalize off their slavery.

JOT YOUR JOURNEY

QUESTION: What is an enslaved person, and what does that word mean to you?

_____

_____

_____

_____

_____

ANSWER: *A slave is someone who has no rights. They are not protected by the law or by society. They are viewed as property and treated inhumanely.*

★ ★ ★

QUESTION: Why would someone use the term *'trafficking'* rather than slavery?

_____

_____

_____

_____

ANSWER: *The terms 'slavery' and 'trafficking' are used interchangeably and mean the same thing. Trafficking is the preferred verbiage, as it portrays the image of globally transporting or using people (as a commodity) for illegal activities worldwide.*

SLAVES OF TODAY

★ ★ ★

There is a greater demand for products and services around the world, and this is due to the ability to see what is for sale and then purchase it online. Our virtual society has created a desire for trafficking like never before.

All types of trafficking take advantage of the manipulated and controlled individual. They are treated inhumanely by the person they serve or who purchases them.

EXPLOITATION is the act in which someone mistreats another individual to benefit from their oppression. Those who are exploited are targeted by those who benefit from their lowly position. Exploitation is the heartbeat of slavery.

JOT YOUR JOURNEY

QUESTION: Do you want to be a trafficked slave?

_____

_____

_____

_____

ANSWER: *Modern-day slaves that are trafficked are subject to abuse, used as a commodity, and are often killed. They are treated with no regard for their feelings, pain, and humiliation; and usually suffer vast amounts of trauma. Only 1% of enslaved people are ever rescued! No one wants or deserves to be enslaved.*

⭐ ⭐ ⭐

QUESTION: Why do those poor in finances or spirit become an easy target for exploitation?

_____

_____

_____

_____

ANSWER: *Traffickers target those who are underprivileged in order to gain the upper hand over them. Exploiters will promise the vulnerable a better life on the contingency that they submit to the opportunities they bring. Those who don't have financial, physical, or emotional needs have no reason to trust and partner with a trafficker - and they know it.*

TRAFFICKING METHODS

★ ★ ★

Experts recognize that three main tactics lure unsuspecting victims into trafficking.

FORCE - **overpowering** someone to be enslaved.

FRAUD - **tricking** someone into being enslaved.

COERCION - **manipulating** someone to be enslaved.

These tactics are always used and often overlap when luring newly enslaved people into the market. Learning about the different tactics used in force, fraud, and coercion can save an unsuspecting victim from the deceptive clutches of trafficking.

JOT YOUR JOURNEY

QUESTION: What three ways do predators lure individuals into the slave trade?

_____

_____

_____

_____

ANSWER: *Traffickers use force, fraud, and coercion.*

★ ★ ★

QUESTION: Why do you think different methods are used to lure victims into the slave trade?

_____

_____

_____

ANSWER: *Traffickers use varying tactics in specific parts of the world to trap slaves in the trafficking market. They intend to make a profit off of human souls. They adjust their tactics for different parts of the world based on an individual's culture and society, usually baited with the lure of a better life.*

Force

⭐ ⭐ ⭐

FORCE - **overpowering** someone to be enslaved.

Traffickers use **FORCE** to get their victims in the slave trade by using brut strength. Sadly, the force doesn't stop when the victim is in bondage.

Traffickers do horrific things to keep their targeted servants submissive through beatings and torture. Physical enforcement is expected in slavery, as the victim usually has no choice but to comply if they want to survive.

This specific tactic is often found among traffickers because it strips the victim powerless and forces them to submit. Victims of force trafficking are usually terrified and comply out of fear of punishment and threats. This form is easier to identify in victims as they are typically broken down in fear.

JOT YOUR JOURNEY

QUESTION: Someone kidnaps you, and before you know it, you are laboring in a mine and can't escape. If you try to leave, they whip you. Since you want to survive, you must continue working for those who are lording over you. What has happened?

_____

_____

_____

_____

ANSWER: *You have been trafficked by force into labor trafficking.*

⭐ ⭐ ⭐

QUESTION: While you were sleeping, someone stole you from your bed. You wake up to discover that you have been shipped to China to be sold. You are starved, beaten, and stripped from everything you own, including any identification to verify your citizenship. You realize that you will never make it back home and will be sold to the highest bidder as a wife. To stop the beatings and starvation, you comply. You stand on the auction block in utter helplessness. What has happened?

_____

_____

_____

_____

ANSWER: *You have been trafficked by force into bride trafficking.*

FRAUD

FRAUD - **tricking** someone into enslavement.

Traffickers may use **FRAUD** to pull victims into the slave trade by using manipulation, lies, and mental confusion. Traffickers will go to great lengths to ensure that their targets remain submissive through various means of fraud. Psychological manipulation is common in slavery; victims are tricked into situations and circumstances out of control.

Fraud usually strips the victim of any real awareness of the circumstances, and they become helpless of any escape. Unable to know what's happening, victims are unequipped to escape the situation they unwittingly entered. Because deception has been created around them, they often cannot recognize the dangerous situation until it is too late.

JOT YOUR JOURNEY

QUESTION: Someone comes up to you and gushes about your beauty. They offer you an all-expenses paid trip to L.A. for a job interview as a model. You excitedly take the opportunity to visit California. But when you get there, you are met by three men who sell you to a brothel. You realize that you have been tricked and can't leave. What has happened?

_____

_____

_____

ANSWER: *This is trafficking by fraud into sex trafficking.*

QUESTION: You are from a small, poor town and desire to make a better life for yourself. It seems like an answer to prayer when you are offered work at a high-end restaurant. You agree and travel to another city. But when you get there, you are beaten, and they break both of your legs. The men that hit you say you have to beg on the streets as a disabled person and bring them whatever money is made. What has happened?

_____

_____

_____

_____

ANSWER: *This is trafficking by fraud into beggar trafficking.*

COERCION

COERCION - **manipulating** someone to be enslaved.

Traffickers may use **COERCION** to get their victims in the slave trade by using mental manipulation. Traffickers will go to great lengths to study their targets and act on various means of coercion through blackmail, extortion, and threats to subdue their victims. This approach is common among traffickers to get their victims into hopeless situations and circumstances they can't escape.

Coercion is a common theme woven throughout trafficking because it uses threats and intimidation to keep victims submissive to traffickers for a lifetime. Coercion also uses the victim's guilt in a situation to keep them there.

JOT YOUR JOURNEY

QUESTION: Passing by a sign that says a hospital will pay you $100 to be a blood donor, you go in and discover that you have a rare blood type. Then you are approached to do the service off-site for an extra $400. You reluctantly decide that you are willing to take the risk because you want the money. You meet a new doctor and sit down to give blood. But when you wake up in pain, you realize that you have been drugged and find yourself covered in blood. What has happened?

_____

_____

_____

_____

ANSWER: *You have been coerced with fraud into organ trafficking.*

⭐ ⭐ ⭐

QUESTION: You meet a cute guy who asks for some sexy selfies. You sext some pictures and send them off. But then he blackmails and threatens you that he will release them to your family unless you have sex with him and his friends. What has happened?

_____

_____

_____

_____

ANSWER: *You have been trafficked by coercion into sex trafficking.*

WHAT IS SEX TRAFFICKING?

Sex trafficking is slavery in our society and focuses primarily on sexual services. It is often that victims of sex trafficking are tricked and manipulated into doing sex acts that benefit someone else (usually one they "love"), sometimes convinced that it is only for a short time. They don't know that their trafficker will never let them leave because of the money they bring in.

Sex trafficking can include the methods of force, fraud, or coercion to pull someone into the sex trade. Victims are convinced by their exploiters that doing sex acts for money will be painless and an easy way to earn a living. But they will soon realize that they have been pulled into one of the most tortuous forms of slavery today.

JOT YOUR JOURNEY

QUESTION: You are blackmailed and bullied into having sex with someone you don't want to, but you can't seem to get out of it and comply with the situation. What has happened?

_____

_____

ANSWER: *You have been sex trafficked through coercion and force.*

QUESTION: Someone offers you a job, but when you arrive, it's apparent that you've been tricked and are pressured into having sex to pay off a debt you owe them. What has happened?

_____

_____

ANSWER: *You have been sex trafficked through fraud.*

QUESTION: Someone convinces you to sell your body for sex and give the money to them. But afterward, you realize that you have been manipulated into complying. What has happened?

_____

_____

ANSWER: *You have been sex trafficked through fraud and coercion.*

SEX TRAFFICKING BY FORCE

Sex trafficking through **FORCE** is typically what people think of when first learning about sexual slavery. Images might come to mind of those powerless to leave a situation and continue in slavery. If this is what you think trafficking by force looks like, you would be right.

This is a common method used in certain parts of the world where women and children have fewer rights and are less protected. Victims of forced sex trafficking are usually stolen off the streets, kidnapped from their homes, or physically muscled into submission. All this is forced onto innocent victims who live a life of sexual slavery. Bound and forced into slavery, rarely do they escape or have the ability to free themselves due to the overwhelming tactics used to subjugate them.

Jot Your Journey

QUESTION: A little girl is kidnapped from her bed and is sold the next day to a stranger as a household maid and sex slave. In fear, the little girl resists and tries to run away. She gets caught and is beaten until she finally submits as a household slave. How does this describe sex trafficking by force?

_____

_____

_____

_____

ANSWER: *Due to her age, physical weakness, and inability to seek help, this little girl is no match for those who have trafficked her.*

★ ★ ★

QUESTION: A teenage boy is walking from school and is offered a ride home. He gets in the car and is raped by the two men who picked him up. They take the unwilling and terrified teenager to a house where he is locked in a room and then sold to other men for sex. How does this describe sex trafficking by force?

_____

_____

_____

_____

ANSWER: *This young boy doesn't have the physical strength or ability to escape his situation, forcing him to stay.*

FORCED SEX TRAFFICKING

Brothels are notorious for sex trafficking by **FORCE**. The disreputable establishments often have bodyguards, as the owners use force to keep their victims prostituting.

Brothels often have locks on the outside of the doors, ensuring that the victims can not leave or use other means of force to make the victim comply with prostitution demands. Sex trafficked victims placed into these situations by force are often ready to leave their situation immediately.

Those who experience forced sex trafficking suffer vast amounts of trauma due to the inability to escape their encounter with physical and sexual abuse. Stories of "rescuing" victims often come from this type of trafficking due to the victim's eagerness to leave the situation.

JOT YOUR JOURNEY

QUESTION: A brothel in Las Vegas, Nevada, reprimands, punishes, threatens, and fires girls if they refuse to have sex with a customer. Does that sound like sexual freedom for prostitutes, or does this reveal aspects of forced trafficking?

_____

_____

ANSWER: *Prostitutes who work in brothels do not have the freedom of choice to have sex with whomever they want. When money is involved and a third party orchestrates sex buyers - money becomes the whip of submission.*

QUESTION: A brothel in Germany has an order board for different types of sex and other activities to purchase. For a little extra cash, an individual can cut the girl with a knife that has been purchased. How does this reveal sex trafficking?

_____

_____

_____

_____

ANSWER: *An ex-brothel owner in Germany once stated, "I didn't sell sex at my brothel... I sold sexual violence against women." No one has the right to purchase sex, nor do they have the authority to pay a fee to harm others in anyway - including cutting them.*

SEX TRAFFICKING BY FRAUD

Sex trafficking through **FRAUD** is usually strategically played out. A particular scenario is created by the trafficker and implemented in various stages.

Fraud is another term for **TRICKERY**.

Traffickers trick victims into circumstances they would not be in if they were told the whole story. Fraud is often masqueraded as an opportunity to benefit the targeted person, but then traps are set to sell them for sex with the inability to get out.

Traffickers will spend years creating frauded situations that look legit and legal. Sometimes it is hard to tell the difference between a real organization or a forgery.

JOT YOUR JOURNEY

QUESTION: A teenage girl is approached by her neighbor to work for a relative in another town. The adolescent girl runs home, excited about the opportunity to make money working as a house cleaner. Her family agrees and happily sends her off. But when she gets there, she is beaten, raped, and forced to be a household slave for no pay. Unable to know how to return home, she stays. How does this describe sex trafficking by fraud?

_____

_____

_____

_____

ANSWER: *The victim has been tricked and can not escape.*

QUESTION: A teenage boy auditions for an online music contest. He wins and is flown to New York to record his own song. But when he arrives, he is told that he has to pay off the travel expenses by working at a local strip club and having sex with the music managers. He complies. Two years later, he is still unable to pay off the amount. What has happened?

_____

_____

_____

ANSWER: *Through fraud this boy has been sex trafficked.*

FRAUD SEX TRAFFICKING

Sex trafficking by **FRAUD** is common in places around the world where money is tight, and job opportunities are seen as a way out of poverty. Unsuspecting victims believe the offer is good and find themselves in a compromising position. After they enter a trapped situation, they have no options but to submit to the trafficker.

It's also common that victims of fraud have previously agreed to things with the trafficker, and trust was gained through this process. When in fact, the trafficker orchestrated it all. Victims of fraud tend to blame themselves for getting into bad situations. A frauded situation is often complex, as paperwork, documents, and other so-called 'legal ' items are signed to convince the victim they need to stay, making them convinced they should stay.

JOT YOUR JOURNEY

QUESTION: A young girl sees an ad for a marriage opportunity in another country. Always dreaming about the land of opportunity, she pursues the idea by answering the marriage ad, wanting to be loved and provided for. She contacts the number on the poster and is transferred to an agency. The agency appears legit and agreed to cover all the expenses. They included a guarantee that if she didn't like whom she was introduced, she was free to return to her family for no additional cost. Is this agency trustworthy? Should she agree to the terms and answer the ad? What could go wrong?

_____

_____

_____

_____

_____

ANSWER: This *agency uses a typical method to trick girls through fraud. A clear example of sex trafficking by fraud, these traffickers pose as agencies that appear legal and invite victims to contact home and enter their trap. If the girl went along with the agency, she would soon discover that she would be sold to the highest bidder and never return home.*

Sex Trafficking by Coercion

Sex trafficking by **COERCION** is usually coupled with mental manipulation. This introduces the individual to the sex trade and is used to keep the victim in slavery. Prostitution is popularly painted as a highly profitable and viable option for those with few options. But those in prostitution find that the trauma of being a sex slave is never worth any amount of money.

Sex trafficking by coercion is usually in areas around the world where women and children are prostituted. Victims of coercion suffer immense amounts of manipulation by the lure of making money. Coercion is often paired with verbal, emotional, physical, and sexual abuse. The most commonly used method today is coercion, as it convinces the prostituted to stay prostituting.

JOT YOUR JOURNEY

QUESTION: A woman is abducted outside a grocery store and held against her will in a warehouse. The men who stole her proceeded to open their phones, revealing pictures of her family at home, eyeing her 16-year-old daughter. They tell her they will not harm her little girl if she agrees to submit to their demands. They tell her that she can go home, but every Friday and Saturday night, she has to sell herself at a local brothel that the men have owned for two years. Out of fear and desperation to protect her daughter, she travels to the brothel for the next two years and sells herself for a profit she never receives. Accepting her place at the brothel, a sex buyer approaches her and asks why she is there. Constantly remembering the threats to her daughter, she tells the sex buyer she is there of her own free will. How does trafficking by coercion change the motives of those who are prostituted?

_____

_____

_____

_____

_____

ANSWER: *Blackmail and threats are often used in sex trafficking to keep victims silenced, submissive, and afraid of disobeying.*

COERCED SEX TRAFFICKING

Entering the sex trade is popularly presented as a glamorous lifestyle, but it is the opposite that holds true. Prostitution uses the **COERCION** of money to engage in sex acts, making every transaction of prostitution ~ sex trafficking.

Victims of coerced sex trafficking are mentally manipulated to remain in prostitution to make money. Since prostitution targets vulnerable people groups, its victims cannot leave the situation and are forced to serve lifelong sentences to sex buyers in trafficking.

Traffickers are creative and spend years making a situation seem good enough to take the bait. These professional traffickers will spend years solidifying victims so they can make hundreds of thousands off of their bodies.

Jot Your Journey

QUESTION: A homeless man is on the side of the road, drenched from the pouring rain. A friendly-looking guy drives up and offers the homeless man a warm place to sleep and dinner at his house. But there is a contingency. The guy tells the homeless man that he would trade dinner and a warm bed to sleep in - if they have sex. The homeless man, with limited options and extremely hungry, reluctantly agrees. Does this describe sex trafficking by coercion? How so?

_____

_____

_____

_____

_____

_____

ANSWER: *Yes, it does show sex trafficking by coercion. Using the victim's lack of necessities, food, and shelter, forces the individual to make survival decisions and agree to things that he wouldn't normally do - if in different circumstances. This example reveals the homeless man in a position of weakness where others can take advantage of his situation, exploiting his poverty through sexual exploitation.*

SEX TRAFFICKING IS SLAVERY

In the past, slavery was marked by a distinctive mindset for subjugated people. They had to submit to slavery and to the masters that oppressed them. Bondage often starts in the mind and is cultivated by those who exercise authority over them. Sadly, those who make money from selling sex slaves desire more enslaved people to obtain a more significant profit. Thus acquiring more slaves is an ongoing marketing strategy to make more money. Sex sells, and because we have an over-sexualized culture, the lust for sex has increased at an alarming rate. Pulling new boys and girls into the sex trade will profit traffickers. But the victims aren't allowed a choice, as they will be forced to have sex with whoever buys them.

JOT YOUR JOURNEY

QUESTION: A young girl has a new boyfriend who promises the world to her. She is swept off her feet and falls in love with him. But throughout the first year of dating, he starts challenging their sexual boundaries, and they begin sleeping together. Two years later, he claims that he'll be homeless if he doesn't get some quick cash. He reluctantly but persistently asks the young girl to prostitute to make him a little money. He persuades her by saying it would only be until he gets back on his feet; she would be doing it for him. Should she agree and prostitute for him and their future together?

_____

_____

_____

_____

_____

ANSWER: *If she decides to prostitute for him, she will never be able to get out. Traffickers will often use relationships to manipulate victims, as they are willing to make emotional decisions tied to love. This is a clear example of sex trafficking and usually a typical situation to coerce a victim into bondage.*

FREE THE SLAVES

Slavery is described as the inability to attain freedom and having no choice in a lifestyle. Using various methods against the victim, by force, fraud, or coercion, pushes an individual into a situation that takes away their freedom.

Whether someone wants to stay in slavery or not is irrelevant. The reality is that freedom is a fundamental human right! This means we must fight for those who are enslaved to be free. World history is full of stories about brave individuals working hard and demanding freedom for slaves. But today, we have more slaves than ever before. Since only 1% of victims are ever rescued from sex trafficking, researchers and abolitionists work hard to gather information from the few survivors, trying to attain knowledge and free more modern-day enslaved people.

JOT YOUR JOURNEY

QUESTION: Lily, young and free at 18 years old, was thrilled to meet an online friend. The new online acquaintance, Elise, encouraged Lily to model. Telling her that she would pay for the flights and let her stay at her house, all Lily had to do was the audition. Excited about the opportunity, Lily flew across the country. Lily and Elise hit it off. Elise paid for shopping trips and food. But a couple of days later, she demanded that Lily pay her back for the flights, shopping excursions, and other expenses she unknowingly accumulated. Unable to pay the amount, Elise told Lily that she must work at a strip club to pay off the debt. Lily tried to find someone to wire the $2,000 but couldn't and reluctantly started working at a strip club to pay her back. But the debt never got paid as housing and food costs increased. Before long, Lily has been stripping for three years and giving all the money to Elise. How is this story an example of sex trafficking?

_____

_____

_____

ANSWER: *This very scenario is played out through many various situations. A victim is selected and flown away from family and friends to be manipulated, pressured, and ultimately dominated. Strip clubs are often the first step to grooming the victim into the sex trade and normalizing their sexual exploitation as they learn to hand the money to their pimp/trafficker for years to come.*

PROSTITUTION IS SEX TRAFFICKING?

Is prostitution sex trafficking? Actually, yes, sex trafficking includes all forms of prostitution. This means that every time a person is bought for sex, they are being trafficked. Sex slavery and prostitution mirror each other. How is prostitution considered sex trafficking? Because every sex buyer is using the coercion of money to entice the person to engage in a sexual act.

Therefore, by definition, every purchased sex act is trafficking. Whether the victim is being compelled to trade sex for money, shelter, food, clothes, or drugs reveals that coercion is at the heart of the sex trade, which strips the victim of choices.

If a trade needs to happen for sex, then coercion has already taken hold of the sex deal, making it a trafficking situation as one with greater power and authority purchases another.

JOT YOUR JOURNEY

QUESTION: A teenage boy was kicked out of his house and found himself sleeping on the streets, alone and cold during a winter storm. He was approached by a young man who encouraged him to prostitute himself to men as an alternative to sleeping on the streets. For the next ten years, he did just that and prostituted himself so he wouldn't be homeless. How does this prove that prostitution is sex trafficking?

_____

_____

_____

_____

ANSWER: *By using the victim's lack of necessities, food, and shelter, it forces an individual to make survival decisions based on the desperate situation they find themselves in. In this scenario, the homeless youth was in a position of weakness, making it easy for others to take advantage of his situation, benefiting from his poverty through his own sexual exploitation. Since trafficking only requires a sex buyer to categorize it as sex trafficking, every time that sex is purchased from the young man and uses the coercion of money for him to engage in a sex act is taking away his choice and his sexual freedom, which is why he can be bought as a sex slave.*

PROSTITUTION

IS KEY

⭐ ⭐ ⭐

How is prostitution the same as sex trafficking? Sex slavery involves limited choices for the victim, as the buyer has the authority to purchase the individual. According to the Federal Trafficking Report in 2019, as in past years, just over half of all victims in criminal human trafficking cases were children. This reveals limited choices and preying on the weak and vulnerable.

The buyer also has ultimate control over the victim they have purchased. A sex buyer once stated, *"The minute I pay for sex, they have no choice... they can't say no when they are with me."* Another sex buyer said, *"Once I put money on the table - they lose all rights and freedoms. I paid for them."* As you can see in the comments of sex buyers, freedom of sexual choice and safety are not considered for the enslaved people.

JOT YOUR JOURNEY

QUESTION: Angela, a 13-year-old, heard from some friends that they went on *Sugar Dates* and were each given a costly purse. Angela went online and signed up for a *Sugar Daddy* date. She was given a room number at a nice hotel to meet up with her *Sugar Daddy*. She was excited to go on a date with an older guy and hoped she would also get a new purse. She didn't want her parents to know, so she lied and told them she was at a friend's house. But when she arrived at the hotel, she was raped. She continued having sex with her *Sugar Daddy* because she was afraid her parents would find out what she had signed up for. The police intervened for minor sex trafficking, and she was rescued - two years later. She reported to the police that she had no idea sex would be involved when she met her *Sugar Daddy* that first day but felt she was too far gone to stop. How does this young girl's story reveal that prostitution is sex trafficking?

_____

_____

_____

ANSWER: *Sugaring uses the coercion of money for girls to engage in sex acts with older men. Prostitution uses racial, gender, social, ethnic, financial, and other prejudices to put the victim at a disadvantage in order to compel and coerce them into sex acts. Any minor (under 18) that engages in sex acts for money is called minor sex trafficking.*

WHAT IS A PIMP?

Sex traffickers are pimps. They sell prostituted victims and make a profit off of their slavery. Pimp is a term equivalent to a sex trafficker, although the term **PIMP** is often glorified.

The word is actually an acronym, "**PERSON INTO MARKETING PROSTITUTES**." Or, as an FBI agent revealed to us what they like to use, "Power In Manipulating Prostitutes."

Pimps, aka traffickers, market prostitutes and sell them to buyers, making a profit from selling a human being. Prostitutes don't need a pimp, but pimps need prostitutes... Think about it.

It is perfectly acceptable to use the terms interchangeably, as they both signify a person who makes a profit from individuals who are sold for sex. On the street and in the life, the term **PIMP** is used; however, in advocacy work, rescue operations, undercover police endeavors, recovery programs, and abolition efforts, the term **TRAFFICKER** is used instead.

JOT YOUR JOURNEY

QUESTION: Jen moves into an apartment with her new boyfriend, Brian. But Brian can't make the payments, and they soon find themselves homeless. He introduces Jen to an old friend who prostitutes. Jen talks to this new individual about her 'work' and asks Brian if she should prostitute to get off the streets. Brian says he will do anything she wants and willingly supports her choice to get them a place. After some consideration, she finally prostitutes and gives Brian the money for rent. Is her boyfriend considered a pimp and sex trafficker?

_____

_____

_____

_____

ANSWER: *Actually, the answer is yes. This tactic is often used in countries with laws stating that the idea of prostitution has to come from the victim, which clears all charges of the trafficker. Victims don't realize that the stage has been set for the girl to feel obligated, by having survival needs, to prostitute herself through homelessness. The trafficker disguises himself as a boyfriend and coerces his target to be a loyal subject for profitable gain. In this scenario, Brain also introduced his target to a victim of sexploitation to coerce Jen into prostitution. This prime example shows how pimps often convince their victims to prostitute by using circumstances, poverty, and homelessness to manipulate them into being sex slaves.*

FULL OF FEAR

Pimps are a big part of the problem because they are committing crimes against humanity, as they are modern-day slave owners. **TRAFFICKERS** (pimps) kidnap, lie, manipulate, threaten, and coerce victims into the seXXX trade. Some will threaten and beat innocent individuals demanding submission under the penalty of torture. Other traffickers create trauma-bonding to subdue their victims and make them compliant as a slave with no chains, yielding to their authority. Pimps can be of either gender and use fear to keep their victims controlled.

Traffickers will then sell these victims to brothels, individual buyers, the black market, or even keep them as their property; inevitably, they will be beaten, raped, and forced to do sexual acts in exchange for money. Many victims of trafficking come forward and reveal the fear of punishment if they ever leave.

JOT YOUR JOURNEY

QUESTION: What would someone have to do to make you compliant with selling yourself for sex?

_____

_____

_____

_____

ANSWER: *Victims of sex trafficking have reported many crimes being committed against them from their pimps. These include: being raped, assaulted, burned with a blow torch, choked, hit with bats and guns, dragged across the room by their hair, beaten, heads slammed into walls, kicked while pregnant, punched in the face, weapons being used against them, stabbed, tortured, slapped, abducted, sent to hospitals with broken bones and put into comas, locked in trunks, shaved heads, left for dead, dragged behind cars, and even had their feet run over with a car.*

⭐ ⭐ ⭐

QUESTION: Aside from the abuse, how much money does a trafficker/pimp expect the victim to make each night?

_____

_____

_____

ANSWER: *Victims of sex trafficking report 'quotas' that they have to bring their pimp, ranging anywhere from $1,000 to as high as $4,000 a night. They will be' disciplined' if they don't bring back their quota.*

PROSTITUTED VICTIMS

★ ★ ★

If the victims don't submit to prostitution, they will be manipulated, abused, tortured, and threatened by their trafficker until they comply. The victim then capitulates into giving over their body to be sold, and the money earned will be given to the trafficker. In the end, it is the traffickers (pimps) who become wealthy. It is the trafficker who deserves to be arrested for privatizing slaves and selling them for sex to slave renters.

Prostitutes are the victims of mental, verbal, physical, sexual, psychological, and spiritual abuse. They need to be rescued and rehabilitated. A common thread between every sexually abused victim is that they have been sexually exploited and used by others and are often coerced into submission. They are indeed the ones that deserve our compassion, as they need help in gaining their freedom from a life of bondage.

JOT YOUR JOURNEY

QUESTION: Interestingly enough, every sex trafficked and prostituted survivor I have talked to was forced to bring in over a thousand dollars a day. If this wasn't accomplished, they would endure torture, discipline, and other horrific things from their trafficker. Does this affect the prostitute's ability to deny a buyer?

_____

_____

_____

ANSWER: *Yes, the trauma and continual cycles of fear, abuse, and control prohibit the prostitute to make any personal choices or sexual preferences. Prostitution reveals a system of oppression, force, fraud, and coercion in exchange for sex for an eluding sense of safety and freedom.*

QUESTION: Charlie, a teenage boy, chats online with a gaming buddy who tells him he can make easy money. Charlie agrees to meet him. A man shows up and takes the teenage boy to a house where he is sold to other men for sex. After 4 hours, the terrified boy is given $50. Are boys trafficked for sex too?

_____

_____

_____

_____

ANSWER: *Yes, boys make up about 2% of those who are prostituted.*

A New Understanding

It has been recently understood that trafficking is much more intricate than previously thought, hence why the terms have changed. Sex trafficking is the term for prostitution whenever there is force, fraud, or coercion involved (which is a constant theme according to research and victim interviews).

Thanks to the concerted efforts made in research and development in social justice, it's now realized that prostitution isn't as voluntary as was previously thought. We are starting to see and understand the invisible chains that have bound these victims. This brings new aspects of the seXXX trade previously hidden in the dark. This creates a new mindset to fight human injustice and new terms to categorize the corruption of human slavery.

JOT YOUR JOURNEY

QUESTION: A father orchestrated sex buyers for his son when he turned seven years old. The little boy had no idea what was in store when he visited his dad for the weekend. The little boy grew up being sold for sex for years in silence. Is the father considered a pimp and a sex trafficker?

_____

_____

_____

_____

ANSWER: *Sadly, yes. Familial trafficking is popular, as they use their kids to make money, business deals, and drug trades. All parties involved, minus the child victim, are guilty of minor sex trafficking.*

⭐ ⭐ ⭐

QUESTION: A boyfriend suggests that his girlfriend should prostitute to buy a house. The girlfriend decides to do it for their future, and he collects the money to 'save' it for their future home together. Is the boyfriend considered a sex trafficker?

_____

_____

_____

ANSWER: *Yes! The boyfriend has become her sex trafficker. This is an excellent example of how pimps often convince their girlfriends to prostitute, using dreams to manipulate one into being a sex slave.*

ENSLAVING THE YOUTH

★ ★ ★

Some say that the average age of those entering into prostitution is as young as twelve.[1] Others say the average age is a year or two older.[2] But no matter if the age is twelve, thirteen, or fourteen, this is the average age of entry into prostitution. But why children? Traffickers acquire younger persons because they are easier to manipulate, dominate, and sell. Children are defenseless from being beaten, controlled, or owned.

When children grow up in the 'LIFE' of slavery, they have been conditioned to accept their situation. Their lot in life of being sold for sex becomes a 'normal' way of thinking, and they take it with them into adulthood. Therefore, an older prostitute in the 'LIFE' is usually evidence of a grown child who was coerced into the sex trade.

JOT YOUR JOURNEY

QUESTION: Who is easier to manipulate and control, an eleven-year-old or a thirty-year-old? Why?

_____

_____

_____

_____

ANSWER: *A child is always easier. Why go after a guarded adult when vulnerable and ill-equipped children are much easier to manipulate?*

⭐ ⭐ ⭐

QUESTION: Why has sex trafficking become such a massive problem worldwide?

_____

_____

_____

_____

ANSWER: *Human trafficking is fast becoming the largest illegal criminal activity worldwide! But how? And why? Well… How many times can a drug be sold? **Only once**. How many times can an individual sell a gun? **Only once**. But a person can be sold for sex **over** and **over** and **over** and **over** again. Therefore, the selfish gain of those who participate in illegal activities have switched from guns and drugs to focusing on prostitution as a way to make millions.*

SEX BUYERS

Sex buyers are often called '**JOHNS**.' It has been rumored that the name 'John' was given by sex buyers when questioned by the police after being caught with a prostitute. The name stuck. Johns call themselves '**MONGERS**.' Sex buyers are personally fueling billions of dollars into the sex industry.

Advocates now realize that the abuse and mistreatment by johns further bury a prostituted victim deeper into the coffin of hopelessness, helplessness, and despair. Research has shown that johns treat prostitutes deplorably, all because buyers feel they have the right and entitlement to mistreat them since they have **paid** for sex.

One sex buyer stated, *"Being with a prostitute is like having a cup of coffee, when you're done, you throw it out."*[3]

JOT YOUR JOURNEY

QUESTION: How do you think buyers treat prostituted victims?

ANSWER: *Victims have reported many crimes done against them by johns. Their statements include: being raped, assaulted, kicked while pregnant, burned with cigarettes, choked with wire, hit with bats, dragged across the room by their hair, beaten, heads slammed into walls, punched in the face, stabbed, tortured, zip-tied to a bed, slapped, abducted, sent to hospitals with broken bones and put into comas, choked, locked in trunks, shaved heads, left for dead, and even dragged behind cars. Victims of prostitution are left with permanent damage or don't survive because of murder.*

QUESTION: What happens when a prostituted victim tells a buyer they won't do something?

ANSWER: *I interview a survivor, who told a sex buyer that she wouldn't do certain sexual things with him. She was then beaten, zip-tied to the bed, and raped... Afterward, he left no money to take to her pimp, so she had to go out and make more money that night.*

SLAVE RENTERS

A sex buyer, who rents slaves by the hour, had a statement about a prostitute's obligation to comply with anything he chooses to do to her, "*She gives up the right to say no.*" Another john revealed, "*I paid for this. She has **no rights**. She's with me now...*"[4]

Does she have no rights? No citizen or human rights? Is this not **SLAVERY defined**? It seems that somehow prostitutes in our society are no longer citizens of the country that they live in. They are no longer protected by laws or even valued by society. Buyers *coerce* the prostituted with money, which by definition describes sex trafficking. Every human purchased for prostitution has been sex trafficked. Buyers are the ones who are happily raping the enslaved. The buyers need to be arrested, convicted, educated, and rehabilitated.

Jot Your Journey

QUESTION: With incomprehensible mistreatment from sex buyers and traffickers, how is a prostituted victim supposed to handle all the abuse, especially if the exploitation and ill-treatment began as a child - often as young as eleven years old?

_____

_____

_____

ANSWER: *With the cycle of violence and constant hopelessness of never escaping that lifestyle, it is reported that prostitutes have a mortality rate 40 times higher than the average person.[5]*

⭐ ⭐ ⭐

QUESTION: Can a prostituted victim simply leave the sex trade whenever they want?

_____

_____

_____

ANSWER: *92% of prostitutes have been reported saying that they wanted out of the seXXX trade '**immediately**' but couldn't get out.[6] I dare say that the other 8% simply stopped dreaming of freedom. Every prostituted victim I have met all wanted out of the sex trade at one time or another. The truth is, prostitutes can't just leave the lifestyle that allows pimps to make upwards of $30,000 a week.[7]*

CREATING
A PRO

⭐ ⭐ ⭐

How does one become a prostituted victim? In a nutshell, a vulnerable subject is stalked, chosen, and broken down through manipulation, violence, and trauma. Survival skills kick in as submission is accepted by the victim, and eventually, they begin selling themselves for the financial gain of the trafficker. Stories told by prostituted victims reveal horrible acts of violence done against them in order for traffickers to gain complete control.

This is the most precise picture of *Stockholm syndrome*, as victims must submit to and depend on their abuser to stay alive. The term **'TRAUMA-BONDING'** best describes the reliance on the perpetrator who is causing the trauma in order to survive, as their life depends on their trafficker's mercy.

JOT YOUR JOURNEY

QUESTION: A young girl was tricked by a pimp into believing he was her boyfriend. When he got angry and abusive, she complied with all of his biddings, hoping his cruel mistreatment would stop if she obeyed. She agreed to prostitute for him, believing that he would eventually let her stop. Learning what you have about sex trafficking, does this scenario reveal her ability ever to escape prostitution? Why or why not?

_____

_____

_____

_____

_____

ANSWER: *As she obeys her pimp, she believes his abuse will discontinue because of her submission. But this also means that if she ever resists his authority in the future, his rage and abuse will escalate until she is completely broken in spirit - forever being indebted to him. Obedience is constantly tested with the new prostitute as they learn to become subordinate through more and more abuse. Years and years of indoctrination will control a victim's submission. This will result in a trusted slave without the need for chains, and she will remain his lucrative investment. She will never be allowed to leave his grasp, as she will continue to be forced to make his money.*

STOP THE VIOLENCE

Violence is a way of life for a prostitute. The pimp continues to use brutality, force, coercion, substance abuse, false promises, torture, blackmail, and manipulation to control their victims. Traffickers play a psychological game to possess physical and mental control over their victims.[8] The prostituted victim eventually trades her safety, body, and personal freedom for the hopes of survival.

Pimps target vulnerable and insecure girls to sexually exploit. An ex-pimp once said, *"It's impossible to protect girls from the guys like I was. Because that is what we do. We eat, drink, and sleep, thinking of ways to trick young girls into doing what we want them to do."*[9]

This psychological war is at the heart of prostitution. And sadly, if we don't know about it, how can we protect the innocent and fight for their freedom? We can't. And that is why abolitionists today work so hard to change the mentality.

JOT YOUR JOURNEY

QUESTION: What kind of victims are traffickers looking for?

_____

_____

_____

ANSWER: *Victims of sex trafficking are often young, vulnerable, and in need of love and acceptance. Traffickers encourage them to objectify and exploit themselves sexually. Did you know that 95% of modern-day prostitutes admit to being sexually abused as a child?[10] In this toxic cycle of abuse, children grow up with the normality of abuse. I dare say that prostitution is just sexually exploiting those who have already been sexually abused. Traffickers find these types of individuals because they can be mentally manipulated to stay in their grasp. Since prostitution targets the vulnerable, it makes victims unable to leave their situation and serve lifelong sentences in trafficking.*

QUESTION: Did you know... **Prostitutes are the most raped class of women in the history of our planet.**[11] What do you think of this?

_____

_____

ANSWER: *This is why sex trafficked victims need our help, support, and voice to end modern-day sex trafficking and all prostitution.*

58

PIMPS

DON'T BLUFF

★ ★ ★

A young teenager rescued from the American seXXX trade revealed what happened when she told her pimp that she wanted to leave. He threatened that if she ever left him, he would kidnap her 11-year-old little sister from her bed and force her into prostitution as her replacement. Because of these threats and her desire to save her little sister, she stayed in prostitution for many more years. She was only 13 years old at the time.[12]

These pimps aren't bluffing either. There are records of pimps doing horrible things to keep their trafficked victims submissive, such as raping, shooting, stabbing, burning, torturing, pulling out fingernails, urinating in their mouths and making them drink it, and all this entirely to keep them in a continual state of fear and submission.[13]

JOT YOUR JOURNEY

QUESTION: Why does a victim comply with prostitution?

_____

_____

_____

_____

ANSWER: *One study shows that the average prostituted victim is raped 16 times a year by her pimp alone.[14] With mental manipulation and extreme violence holding the reins of the seXXX trade, it is only a matter of time before the young, weakened victim succumbs to her new life of madness out of sheer exhaustion and desperation. Starting generally at a young age (12-14), this world becomes a new normal, and any hope for an average life becomes as faded as the hope for value, worth, and love. This withering hope dims more every year as the average lifespan of a prostituted victim is only 3-7 years.[15]*

★ ★ ★

QUESTION: Why is it essential for a pimp to keep 'his girl' under complete control and dominance?

_____

_____

_____

_____

ANSWER: *If he can keep her in a state of fear, he can have a lifelong, obedient slave making him hundreds of thousands of dollars every year.*

IS PROSTITUTION A CHOICE?

★ ★ ★

It is often promoted that prostitution is a choice for those who love sex. Sadly, that is as silly as saying that those who are victims of labor trafficking love hard work and those who are exploited because they are poor - just love their poverty.

We have had decades of the media conditioning us that *sex sells*. This reveals a law of money and power behind whatever is being sold. If sex sells, it is because there is a market for it, which reveals that slavery still exists. Do you think a sex buyer has the right to purchase a human for rape? And yet, it happens every day in the life of a sex trafficked victim. We need to understand that you can't purchase someone for sex. To buy sex is to take away their choice of saying 'no' and puts them in a submissive position under the authority of the purchaser.

Jot your journey

QUESTION: In our society, what do you think about prostitution being promoted as a choice?

_____

_____

_____

ANSWER: *I once asked a survivor (who was sex trafficked for 15 years) about her opinion of women in prostitution who expressed that they 'choose to do it.' She stated, "We all would tell ourselves that we chose this lifestyle. It is the only way to convince ourselves that we want to be there and not go crazy. The truth is, no one wants to be sold. Behind every girl that states, 'I choose to do it,' if you take the time, you will find a past riddled with sexual abuse, and in the very dark background - near the beginning - is a man who started it all..."*

★ ★ ★

QUESTION: What do you think the average life expectancy is for those who are prostituted and sold for sex?

_____

_____

_____

ANSWER: *The conjecture is that victims of sex trafficking have a life expectancy of only 3-7 years, creating a very high risk of death due to rape, torture, beatings, suicide, drug overdose, wounds, and murder.*

SLAVERY IS NOT A PROFESSION

★ ★ ★

In 1991, police in southern California **closed** all rape reports made by prostitutes, placing them in a file stamped *"NHI."* The acronym *"NHI"* stands for *"No Human Involved."*[16] This proves that modern-day slavery still exists as we have entire people groups who are not protected by our laws of humanity.

If we did **not** have prostitution, there would be **no** such thing as sex trafficking. If we could **eliminate** prostitution, then we could **eliminate** sex trafficking. Prostitution and sex slavery are not empowering! Instead, it reveals discrimination against those being purchased, which is degrading and dehumanizing - not empowering.

LAST TIME I CHECKED... SLAVERY IS NOT A PROFESSION.

Jot Your Journey

QUESTION: When the police in southern California **closed** all rape reports made by prostitutes, they placed them in a file stamped *"NHI."*[16] How does this prove that modern-day slavery still exists and that prostitutes are viewed as *'inhuman'*?

_____

_____

_____

_____

ANSWER: *It seems that society has chosen to continue to ignore the brokenhearted. We must no longer turn away from those who desperately need our assistance, mercy, help, rescue, and rehabilitation.*

⭐ ⭐ ⭐

QUESTION: Can sex trafficking be eliminated without eradicating prostitution? Why or why not?

_____

_____

_____

ANSWER: *No. You must eliminate both of them. Prostitution is linked to sex trafficking in more ways than one. In fact, prostitution has a thick thread tied to trafficking, walking hand in hand, arm in arm. They dance together in a beautiful array of distortion, oppression, exploitation, and violence. Sex trafficking includes prostitution, and buyers of prostitution purchase sex trafficked victims.*

WE WERE WRONG...

For decades, lies about prostitution have been believed, and it has shaped our inability to put a stop to human trafficking. And because of this, trafficking has increased.

In the past, we thought...

Prostitutes were the problem.

Pimps were invisible.

Johns (sex buyers) were innocent.

But thanks to the concerted efforts made in research and development, we have learned something very polarizing.

Instead, what we have learned to be true is...

Prostitutes are the victims.

Pimps are masterminding slavery.

Johns (sex buyers) are guilty of buying human slaves.

Sadly, in the past, we believed that prostitutes were the problem. However, modern research reveals that prostituted victims are actually involved in a psychological war that we were unaware of. And since we didn't know about it, we were unable to help them and lacked the means to end slavery.

HARRIET TUBMAN once stated,

*"I freed a thousand slaves. I **could have freed** a thousand more if only they **knew** they were slaves..."*

So some were slaves but didn't know they were slaves? How is that possible? This occurred through the process of education, manipulation, and psychological conditioning. This same psychological manipulation and conditioning used in the past are being used today by pimps and traffickers to keep their victims bound in the sex trade. PIMPS (Person Into Marketing Prostitutes) orchestrate and mastermind a psychological war to ensure that their prostituted victims remain as submissive slaves.

Pulling victims into the sex trade may have many forms, but mental manipulation and coercion is the most common method to control those being sexually exploited. This is done primarily by creating a new family unit. Initially captivating the victim with love, acceptance, and happiness, a new relationship blossoms through affirmation, approval, and welcoming them into an emotional or romantic love affair.

Modern slave owners (aka pimps or traffickers) know how to control and manipulate their victims through abuse, blackmail, threats of violence, torture, drugs, and emotional trauma. Usually, the victim will be unaware that they are a target to be sold until it is too late. Thankfully, with the education of signs to be aware of, victims and families can now be mindful of the tactics used to secure lifelong 'volunteer' sex slaves. To some, it might appear to be 'volunteer' prostitution, but the evidence now suggests that there is no such thing...

As once stated by Johann von Goethe, *"The best slave is one who thinks he is free."* Why? Because they never think of leaving the slavery that they are in and never beg for help to be freed.

This is the mentality that is promoted among prostituted victims today. But why? And how did this happen? Why do victims stay silent? Like abusive and dysfunctional families, pimps (traffickers) mimic these broken family units by conditioning the victim with guilt and fear. In addition, they create family loyalty, one that keeps secrets hidden and will never betray each other as a duty to that allegiance. This mentally keeps the victim silent and prepares them to accept the sexual abuse that will be their act of service to this new relationship or family unit. Secrecy and loyalty are constantly conditioned into the minds of the victims so that the silence can keep their traffickers out of prison. The victims will view their loyalty as an act of love towards their trafficker. Convinced that they are free - **they stay**.

Just because prostituted victims have accepted their lot in life and complied with the demands of their trafficker for survival doesn't mean they are free. In reality, they are abused, tortured, and aren't permitted to leave the 'profession.' After years and years of abuse, these victims have mentally accepted their circumstances of utter ruin and cannot fight for freedom. Again, convinced that they are free - **they stay**. Is this not slavery defined? Let's stand up and fight for those who have no voice and let them know that they, too, can one day be **free**.

JOT YOUR JOURNEY

QUESTION: A young man is musically talented and posted an online video of him singing a local hit. A music producer messaged him and stated that his talent was just what he was looking for and wanted to meet him for an audition. The music producer even offered to pay all traveling expenses. The young man was excited to take the opportunity and flew out to meet him. But after the young man arrived and auditioned, the music producer stated that he would have to pay for the accumulated expenses. Unable to give him thousands of dollars, the young man agreed to be sold for sex until he could pay the debt. Two years later, the young man was still paying off the debt through sexual bondage. How does this *appear* to be 'volunteer' prostitution but reveals sex trafficking by fraud?

_____

_____

_____

_____

ANSWER: *This is actually based on a true story of a young man who was coerced into sex trafficking at 17 years old. Years later, he realized that he was a victim of sex trafficking and his recovery is still in process. Prostitution is linked to sex trafficking in more ways than one. Prostitution has a thick thread tied to many victims who will be scarred for years to come.*

PROTECT THE KIDS

An excited mom posted an image of her son, Darrin*, in front of the school for his first day of kindergarten. She didn't know that her niece had befriended a trafficker on Facebook who had initially targeted her. Once her niece had hearted the picture of Darrin, the trafficker could see her son's picture and the name of the school he would be at every day. Traveling to the area and finding the school, Darrin was met by a man who knew his name and told him that his mom wanted home. So the trafficker picked Darrin up.

We don't know what happened to Darrin after that day, but with an increase of over 774% of online child porn images and videos, we have evidence that children are pulled into trafficking.[33] Sadly, child porn is evidence of minor trafficking.

But it isn't just Facebook that's used. It is every digital, social media platform where traffickers can be in contact with a child. We must teach our children that they are being **hunted**, lured, **coerced**, tricked, and **manipulated** into prostitution. Apps are an excellent way for traffickers to get an introduction to our girls and then prey on them to be potential victims and lifetime captives.

We must educate and warn those we love that those online relationships might not be what is initially assumed. A romantic relationship is a vast arena to acquire young girls into the trafficking world through prostitution. With images of Cinderella in most girls' minds, the idea of an older boy finding them beautiful is enough for any young female to be swept off her feet. We must remember and teach kids that what is being posted online can reveal a vulnerability to their emotional state. They disclose that they are insecure if they constantly post selfies, negative remarks about themselves, dieting, body image, and loving feedback. Unaware, they invite 'prince charming' to meet their needs of love and affirmation.

kik. Rebecca* got a phone for her 14th birthday. She downloaded Kik, an app that her friends were constantly on. She didn't know that Kik's messaging app was also used as a sexting and hook-up tool. Within two months, she was being pursued by a nineteen-year-old guy whose profile picture melted her heart. He texted her often, telling her she was beautiful and asking to see photos of her pretty face.

He started asking for pics of her in her bathing suit, to which she complied. She told him no when he asked for photos of her in her bra and underwear. But he reminded her that it was no different from a bathing suit and told her not to be shy. She was unaware that he was breaking down her moral walls, and slowly she agreed. Aside from the pictures, she also started pouring her heart out to him. She started telling him that she didn't have a great relationship with her parents, wishing she could spend more time with him. Seeing the opportunity, he reminded her that he would love to spend some real-time with her in person. His asking turned into begging...

One night she got into a fight with her parents and told him she wanted to meet him. She didn't know he was a twenty-nine-year-old trafficker using a fake profile and was waiting for his opportunity. He met up with her, kidnapped her, and sold her to gangs in California. It was four years before an undercover police raid rescued her. We only know her story... because she is alive to tell it. With only 1% of trafficked victims recovered, the stories we hear from survivors are few. But thankfully, she was one of those rescued.

But it isn't just girls getting tricked and hunted, but the boys too. Boys have become an increased commodity in the trafficking world. Pedophiles desire to have images of naked young boys and purchase them from traffickers. What was once a hidden fetish is now promoted on the dark web and fueled through online forums on the clear web. Traffickers wish to provide supplies to their buyers.

Today, boys are on the menu. Apart from apprehending runaway children, traffickers have found more efficient ways. Technology has become the wave of the future. With so many boys online, it's easier to hunt those unaware that they are being preyed upon.

 Mikey* started chatting with a girl named Sara* on Snapchat. Two years older, she was beautiful, and he couldn't believe that she found him irresistible. Even though he considered himself a nerd, Sara liked him, and they hit it off, chatting every night. It didn't take long for a meeting to take place. Mikey snuck out at night to meet her at the local park. But when he arrived, she wasn't alone. Sara was also being trafficked and was a 'spotter.' Her job was to locate more victims and introduce them to her trafficker. That night, Mikey was raped by Sara's trafficker and three other men. Devastated afterward, Mikey ran home and climbed into his bed. Crying to sleep, he didn't know what to do and was afraid of getting in trouble for sneaking out of the house.

When he awoke, he received a message from Sara. She stated that he had to meet with her trafficker again, or she would tell Mikey's parents that he ran out of the house. Mikey kept it a secret because he was afraid of getting in trouble with his parents and believing that all the problems were his fault for sneaking out. Mikey was trafficked for four years from his own house until he was too old to sell. He was only twelve years old when he met Sara for the first time...

 Johnny* loved Instagram. A follower messaged him about his favorite sports team. Eager to answer him back, they started communicating about football and the shared love of the game. Within a year, their friendship grew, snapping all the time. One day Johnny got a message that his Instagram friend would be in town and wanted to meet up at a fast-food restaurant. It seemed safe, as he was another young boy, so they set up a meeting. Johnny never expected to meet a fifty-five-year-old man who had been lying to him for over a year. The trafficker drugged and raped the sixteen-year-old. He then sold the boy for two weeks to sex buyers in the area.

When he let him go, Johnny and his parents went straight to the police. But all the Instagram posts led to an empty profile and no leads. Even though Johnny is no longer being sold, the trauma of trafficking led to heroin addiction, which he is still struggling with as a way to fade the memories.

"IN TODAY'S DIGITAL WORLD, ONE BAD DECISION CAN CHANGE YOUR LIFE."

Opal Singleton, Outreach Coordinator for Riverside County Anti-Human Trafficking Task Force

JOT YOUR JOURNEY

QUESTION: A popular tag from teenagers on Whisper is *"My Parents Cut Me Off Financially For Good."* A young girl recently posted, *"I'm fine. My parents cut me off midway through college with no income and endless bills to pay."* How vulnerable does this young girl appear? And how easy would it be for a trafficker to approach her about making some 'easy' money?

_____

_____

_____

_____

_____

ANSWER: *Sadly, her situation is the perfect storm for her to be coerced into prostitution. She is a perfect target for someone to lure her with hopes of making money. Once the trafficker meets up with her and has traumatized her through torture and rape, she'll become a trapped victim who cannot leave his control. This young woman has no idea that she is an easy target for traffickers by posting things like this. Sadly, this stamps 'vulnerability' on her forehead, along with the information that she and her parents are at odds - a perfect mark. Spotters or traffickers search for opportunities to acquire victims publicly, posting about their vulnerability and insecurity, the two things essential for their control. These social network sites are a perfect source to find new victims and are often used by predators.*

THE DEMAND

Trafficking isn't an issue in certain countries; it's a problem in **every** county. With that said, according to the U.S. State Department report by the New York Times, the United States has become the second most trafficked country in the world[17], as sex trafficking has become a $99 billion dollar industry per year.[17.1] The U.S. Department of Justice reported that 83% of sex slaves were American citizens, some as young as five years old in the United States.[18] But how did we get here? How did this become such a huge problem?

Surprisingly to some, pornography has been the tool used to raise and sustain the supply. Due to the increase in pornography use in this century, the demand for sex trafficking has skyrocketed. Pornography is the same outlet used to document the activities of prostitution and sex trafficking, as it advertises what can be purchased.

Sex Trafficking is the new term used for prostitution, as we realize that trafficking is much more intricate than was previously thought, hence why the term has been adapted.

With that in mind, survivors of sex trafficking are beginning to report that pornography was taken or made of them while they were involved and trapped in trafficking. A sex trafficked survivor once stated, *"Pornography is nothing more than documented abuse."* And because pornography continues to increase in popularity, the demand for sex trafficking will also rise.

PORNOGRAPHY IS A MENU FOR BUYERS.

Think of it this way. Pornography is the menu from which sex buyers order. That's right! Buyers are scrolling online, deciding what they want to see more of and maybe even purchase one day.

Sex trafficking is the second largest criminal activity in the world.[19] It is close to becoming the number one spot due to the demand that pornography creates. Every click increases the demand for pornography; the greater demand, the more supply is needed to meet those demands. But is the activity of pornography that much? Undoubtedly the average person isn't affected by such things!

Contrary to popular belief, a severe but unrecognized epidemic exists today. The regular exposure and consumption of pornography are outrageous! In fact, 98% of men admit to viewing porn regularly, and 73% of women privately confess the same.[20] There are over 40 million Americans who regularly visit porn sites.[21] With so many affected and influenced by pornography, imagine the increase of sex buyers in the future. There are over 28,000 viewers watching porn online every second. This means that every day there are 68 million searches for porn.[22]

We don't understand that pornography cannot be ethically sourced or verified to see if force, fraud, or coercion was involved in the recorded acts of prostitution.

New York Times writer Stephens-Davidowitz writes, "*A shocking number of people visiting mainstream porn sites are looking for portrayals of incest,*" and noted that 16 of the top 100 searches from men seek "*incest-themed videos.*"[23]

Andrea Dworkin said, "*Incest is bootcamp for prostitution.*" As men are seeking to watch sexual assaults between family members, the increase of incest will increase. If that isn't bad enough, there are over 110,000 searches online for child porn every day.[24] People might be outraged at the thought of child porn, but research reveals that 1 out of every five images of all online porn is of a minor.[25]

This means that for all those watching porn, 20% of images they see are of children. This increases the demand for more child porn. With the desire to see children sexually, more children need to be pulled into the sex trade to sexually exploit and capture images of their exploitation. Child pornography, by definition, is child trafficking because a child is forced or coerced to engage in sex acts, the very definition of minor trafficking.

Why is porn the demand for sex trafficking and prostitution?

This is because people want to see new porn, which means fresh victims need to be pulled into the sex trade to record more acts of prostitution - for those viewers. If we can get people to stop looking at porn, we could exponentially decrease the demand for sex trafficking. Maybe even end it!

If the average person stopped viewing porn, the demand would decrease, meaning a lower supply would be needed. And what is the supply? Prostituted and sex trafficked victims. Every 30 seconds, someone becomes a victim of modern-day slavery through trafficking.[26]

But we can change that.

Remember that the average age of those entering trafficking is just 12 years old.[27]

But we can change that too.

The world can be changed by increasing awareness and learning how sex trafficking creates victims. This issue is calling out for advocates and those who will no longer sit on the sidelines. Instead, we must stand up and begin to see that pornography and sex trafficking are increasing due to the silence on this issue.

DECREASING DEMAND

Slavery has been around since the beginning of time. Modern-day slavery, also known as trafficking, has increased at an alarming rate. We know that one of the forms of slavery is sex trafficking. Sex traffickers target vulnerable victims, pulling them into the sex trade to sell them. Today, various anti-trafficking organizations are busy at work trying to rescue and redeem the victimized slaves of today. However, with only 1% of trafficked victims ever rescued, the work is long, tedious, and discouraging.[28] Nevertheless, we must continue fighting to change that number to 100%.

SEX TRAFFICKING IS SEXXX SLAVERY.

Advocates are working hard in research and development to discover 'why' the number of victims is increasing at an alarming rate each year. Sex trafficking is the second largest criminal activity in the world. Why is this? Well, how many times can you sell a gun? Once. How many times can you sell drugs? Once. But they can sell our little girls and boys over and over and over again through sex trafficking.

There's higher profitability for those who exploit victims through sex trafficking. Sadly, it is becoming so popular, as it's an estimated $99 billion dollar a year industry.[29] With the average lifespan of a child or adult engulfed in the sex trade only 3-7 years, the need for more victims is constantly needed, and our children are their desired, endless supply.[30]

But... what is the correlation between modern times and the increase in sex trafficking? What is fueling this giant market? We are discovering that through our newfound *sexual freedom*, our society has created the perfect environment for sexual predators. Our over-sexualized culture became an ideal habitat for the victimization of our youth. We live in a pornified culture that pushes sexualized images and nudity (via music videos, ads, apps, and television).

Our youth are educated by the media to normalize nudity, practice objectification, and accept prostitution. Our children are also taught to sexualize others, creating an environment that welcomes sexual exploitation. Lastly, our youth are introduced to sexualizing themselves, prepping them as objects of sexual oppression and targeting them for sexual exploitation.

What we miscalculated in the evolution of society's *sexual freedom* turned out to be the imprisonment of our very own children. With our kids learning to sexualize others and themselves at such a young age, the ability to coerce them into prostitution is easier than ever. Many aspects pull the strings of trafficking, but with a person entering into trafficking every 30 seconds around the world, we need to slow this down if we want to stop it.[31]

Abolishing slavery in the past was complicated, tedious, and fighting against the culture at the time. Abolitionists in history were brave for going against the progressive aspects of the time and fighting for what was right. Today is no different as we face just as much criticism. Abolitionists and advocates must adhere to that same bravery and tenacity as we struggle against the progressive sexual culture of our day.

HOW CAN WE DECREASE THE DEMAND FOR SEX TRAFFICKING?

Slavery and prostitution have been around for centuries. But it is **not** a coincidence that these two things exist simultaneously. This reveals that they balance and rely on each other for existence. What we need to realize is:

Sexting is practicing pornography.
Pornography is practicing prostitution.
Prostitution is included in sex trafficking.
Sex trafficking is modern-day slavery.

JOT YOUR JOURNEY

QUESTION: An older woman cannot feed her family, so she sells herself to sex buyers to make money. Is it acceptable for her to prostitute herself because she chose it?

_____

_____

_____

_____

ANSWER: *No! Just because someone can sell themselves for sex doesn't make selling or buying sex right. Just because someone wants to sell themselves as a slave doesn't make it right.*

★ ★ ★

QUESTION: A young woman decides to sell herself as a slave. She puts herself for sale online and finds buyers to bid on her. If she is *ok* with selling herself as a slave, why can't we let her? What would be wrong with this?

_____

_____

_____

ANSWER: *We live in a world where slavery needs to be stopped, with no exception. It doesn't matter if someone desires to sell themselves or not. Slavery isn't acceptable even if it has convinced its slaves that they are allowed to be enslaved.*

ABOLISH SLAVERY

If we desire to **ABOLISH** sex trafficking and eradicate slavery, we can't participate, promote, encourage, or practice any of the things that lead up to sexploitation. This means that we are to become intolerant of nudity and objectification, which includes sexting and pornography. We must eradicate sexual objectification in all avenues of our lives, including what we see on a screen.

Prostitution is the heartbeat of trafficking. We realize that prostitutes are coerced into exploiting themselves through traffickers (pimps), dysfunctional family units, childhood abuse, society, media, and our over-sexualized culture. Those who buy sex from prostitutes are indeed buying victims of sex trafficking.

It is also reported that 100% of sex buyers view pornography. Why? Because porn is the documentation of prostitution and sex trafficking is the purchasing of that prostitution.

To eradicate sex trafficking, we must become convinced that we are not allowed to purchase another human being - for anything - including sex.

SLAVERY ISN'T A PROFESSION.

We should **never** promote slavery as an option for those with limited choices. Those selling themselves for survival reasons reveal that they wouldn't be making those choices if they had money and the means to make a better way for themselves. This means that the need for survival puts the victim in a position of weakness. They are then submissive to those who are more wealthy than them and are taken advantage of and exploited. We are supposed to protect the vulnerable, not exploit, profit from, or sell them. Sex should never be for sale.

WE MUST REALIZE THAT WITHOUT PROSTITUTION THERE WOULD BE NO SEX TRAFFICKING.

Since we know what freedom is and are free - we are the ones who are supposed to free those who have accepted their slavery as normal and those who are not free. Slavery isn't right just because one is convinced it is ok to be sold. This is why it is essential to demand freedom for all and resist slavery, even if people want it for themselves. Slavery isn't a choice... and we must teach others never to accept slavery as an option.

So, how do we do our part? We must choose not to objectify anyone and refuse to engage in or accept prostitution. Help eradicate sex trafficking by decreasing demand through becoming intolerant of sexual exploitation and not consuming, engaging, advertising, promoting, normalizing, or desiring any forms of sexual exploitation. By doing this, you will decrease the demand, and you will help end sex trafficking! Through learning about trafficking and its true identity, you can now promote the truth and help **FIGHT TRAFFICKING**.

THANK YOU

FOR LEARNING ABOUT SEX TRAFFICKING AND COMPLETING THE

ABOLITIONIST TRAINING 101

**THROUGH THIS SEX TRAFFICKING
EDUCATIONAL GUIDEBOOK,**

BECAUSE TOGETHER

WE CAN CHANGE THE WORLD.

Cited Information:

* The name and slight information have been changed to protect the identity of individuals.

1. http://www.rapeis.org/activism/prostitution/prostitutionfacts.html
2. Sara Ann Friedman for ECPAT-USA, "Who Is There to Help Us?" 2005
3. Melissa Farley, Emily Schuckman, Jacqueline M. Golding, Kristen Houser, Laura Jarrett, Peter Qualliotine, & Michele Decker, 2011, Comparing Sex Buyers with Men Who Don't Buy Sex: 'You can have a good time with the servitude' vs. 'You're supporting a system of degradation,' Report at Psychologists for Social Responsibility Annual Meeting, Boston.
4. Melissa Farley, 2007, 'Renting an Organ for Ten Minutes:' What Tricks Tell Us about Prostitution, Pornography, and Trafficking. Pornography: Driving the Demand for International Sex Trafficking, Los Angeles: Captive Daughters Media.
5. http://www.rapeis.org/activism/prostitution/prostitutionfacts.html Special Committee on Pornography and Prostitution, 1985, Pornography and Prostitution in Canada 350.
6. Melissa Farley, Isin Baral, Merab Kiremire, Ufuk Sezgin, "Prostitution in Five Countries: Violence and Posttraumatic Stress Disorder" (1998) Feminism & Psychology 8 (4): 405-426)
7. New York Times; Prostitution Isn't as Profitable As You Think by ELIANA DOCKTERMAN, March 12, 2014, https://time.com/21351/prostitution-isnt-as-profitable-as-you-think/
8. https://www.endslaverynow.org/blog/articles/basic-stages-of-grooming-for-sexual-exploitation
9. https://www.youtube.com/watch?v=7xdkNE8Jp9E
10. ISA research and In Plain Sight Documentary & Melissa Farley, 2004, Prostitution is sexual violence. Psychiatric Times.
11. Susan Kay Hunter and K.C. Reed, 1990, "Taking the side of bought and sold rape," Speech at National Coalition Against Sexual Assault, Washington, D.C.
12. Renting Lacy by Linda Smith at Shared Hope
13. https://www.scribd.com/document/337768350/How-Pimps-Train-Bitches-How-Pimps-Break-Bitches-Pimp-Training-Bitches
14. Dr. Melissa Farley Research @ prostitutionresearch.com
15. https://www.jonahproject.org
16. Linda Fairstein, 1993, Sexual Violence: Our War Against Rape, New York: William Morrow and Co.

17. http://libjournals.mtsu.edu/index.php/scientia/article/view/652/595
    1. "Human Trafficking by the Numbers." Human Rights First. Accessed July 31, 2019. https://www.humanrightsfirst.org/resource/human-trafficking-numbers.
18. https://www.state.gov/documents/organization/82902.pdf
19. https://www.unicefusa.org/sites/default/files/assets/pdf/End-Child-Trafficking-One-Pager.pdf
20. https://www.psychologytoday.com/us/blog/experimentations/201802/when-is-porn-use-problem
21. https://www.webroot.com/us/en/resources/tips-articles/internet-pornography-by-the-numbers
22. https://www.kwtx.com/content/news/Waco-ministry-addresses-scourge-of-internet-pornography-addicts-487354401.html
23. https://nypost.com/2017/05/13/google-data-reveals-your-most-perverted-secrets/
24. http://www.techaddiction.ca/files/porn-addiction-statistics.jpg
25. https://www.atg.wa.gov/sex-trafficking
26. http://allworthyoflove.org/human-trafficking/
27. https://www.thefreedomchallenge.com/just-the-facts/
28. www.a21.org/content/human-trafficking
29. https://www.humanrightsfirst.org/resource/human-trafficking-numbers
30. arkofhopeforchildren.org/issues/child-trafficking-statistics
31. http://cityservepdx.org/areas/human-trafficking
32. https://sextraffickingawareness.weebly.com/human-trafficking-facts--statistics.html
33. NCMEC data illustrate the explosion. Child Victim Identification Program
34. The Johns: Sex For Sale and The Men Who Buy It. By Victor Malarek
35. https://www.traffickinginstitute.org/federal-human-trafficking-report-2019/
36. The Johns: Sex For Sale and The Men Who Buy It. By Victor Malarek
37. Catharine A. MacKinnon, 2011, Trafficking, Prostitution, and Inequality, Harvard http://www.prostitutionresearch.com/pdfs
38. Catharine A. MacKinnon, 2011, Trafficking, Prostitution, and Inequality, Harvard http://www.prostitutionresearch.com/pdfs

ABOLITIONIST TRAINING 101

★ ★ ★

30-DAY SEX TRAFFICKING EDUCATIONAL GUIDEBOOK

Please visit www.ISAFreedom.org for more information.

ISBN: 9798506846741

Made in the USA
Monee, IL
14 December 2022